THE
WEDDING SHOWER
BOOK *Second Edition*

THE WEDDING SHOWER BOOK
Second Edition

Janet Anastasio

ADAMS PUBLISHING
Holbrook, Massachusetts

ACKNOWLEDGMENTS

This book would not be complete if we neglected to thank the following people who helped make it possible: Christopher Ciaschini, Susan Beale, Peter Gouck, Lynne Griffin, Mary Hanley, Joanna Hudgens, Lois Kernan, Kate Layzer, Nancy McGovern, Shannon McNeeley, Gigi Ranno, Susan Robinson, and Brandon Toropov.

Published by: Adams Media Corporation
260 Center Street, Holbrook, MA 02343

ISBN: 1-55850-407-9

Printed in Canada

J I H G F E

Library of Congress Cataloging-in-Publication Data
Anastasio, Janet.
   The wedding shower book / Janet Anastasio. — 2nd ed.
      p.   cm.
   Subtitle: How to plan the perfect celebration—including creative ideas for invitations, games, themes, decorations, and more.
   ISBN: 1-55850-407-9
   1. Showers (Parties) 2. Weddings. I. Title.
   GV1472.7.S5A53   1994
   793.2—dc20   94-3728
                                                        CIP

This book is available at quantity discounts for bulk purchases.
For information, call 1-800-872-5627 (in Massachusetts, 781-767-8100).

Designed by Janet Anastasio.
Illustrations by Barry Littmann and Joanna Hodgens.

Table of Contents

Introduction

Pre-Wedding Party

The Wedding Shower Book is a unique guide designed to help you simplify the planning and preparation of pre-wedding parties. Whether you're planning a simple gathering or a sophisticated soiree, you'll find that this book offers a variety of helpful suggestions ranging from shower themes to personally crafted invitations, and from homemade favors to decorations.

A wedding shower is the celebration of a new beginning—a party that will literally "shower" the couple with warm wishes and gifts to help them start a new life together. A popular variant, the pre-wedding shower, allows the couple to meet family and friends from both sides of the family before the wedding.

☙Showers: Changing with the Times

In years past, wedding showers followed a distinct and predictable pattern in nearly all cases. Today, although there are still some broad rules that can be expected to apply to most situations, there is much more diversity.

Traditionally, the maid or matron of honor or good friends of the bride and groom host the shower. Except for certain areas of the country where it is an accepted custom, close relatives, such as the mother of the bride or the siblings, should not host the shower, as this would imply that the family is soliciting gifts. Only people who are invited to the wedding should be invited to the shower. One exception would be a shower held at an office or club for colleagues and acquaintances who probably would not attend the wedding.

A bridal shower today is much different from the ones given by our grandmothers. In many cases nowadays, people getting married are not doing so for the first time—or have been maintaining their own domestic lives for some time and don't need traditional gifts.

Today as more grooms take an active interest in their homes, "co-ed" showers are on the rise. As a result, there is more and more emphasis today on style and presentation in the shower. Is there a theme to the shower? What does the shower say specifically about the future bride and groom? What sort of gifts will make a unique statement about them?

WHEN TO HAVE THE SHOWER

Wedding showers today are most commonly held four to six weeks prior to the wedding, but may be given anytime from two months up to a few weeks before the ceremony. In some cases a shower might even be held a few days in advance of the big event, if that's the only time that long-distance family members and friends will be able to gather before the wedding.

If there's no time for the party before the wedding, that's no reason to panic. It's perfectly all right to give a shower after a couple returns from their honeymoon. Ask the bride what date is most convenient for her. (Surprise showers can be lots of fun, but may backfire when a busy bride suddenly has other plans at shower time!)

Try to choose the time best suited for the principal guests, and do your best to anticipate scheduling problems. In particular:

- Keep in mind the work schedules of those involved, whether during the week or on the weekend, and be sure the majority of guests are able to attend at the time you've selected.
- Remember that on the weekend, many people have errands to run and religious services to attend.
- If you plan to invite children, bear in mind that they may not be able to come during the day on weekdays or late at night.

COUNTDOWN TO A GREAT SHOWER

Whether you are planning a catered dinner for fifty or an intimate gathering of ten, the key to a successful party is careful planning. Don't let yourself become overwhelmed; plan ahead. The difference between a good shower and a great shower is often detail, and the proper level of attention to detail is only possible if you plan ahead. Use the list below as a starting point.

Follow this checklist to help plan the shower. Checking off each task as it is completed leaves you free to concentrate on other details.

Initially:
- ❑ Set time and date for shower.
- ❑ Prepare guest list.

Four to six weeks before the shower:
- ❑ Decide on a theme.
- ❑ Make or buy the invitations.

Three weeks before the shower:
- ❑ Make or purchase any invitations you will need.
- ❑ Start planning the menu and activities.
- ❑ Contact a caterer (if you plan to use one).
- ❑ Begin thinking about prizes you will give away.

Two weeks before the shower:
- ❑ Send out the invitations.
- ❑ Prepare a shopping list.
- ❑ Order a corsage.

One week before the shower:
- ❑ Make a head count of guests who will be attending.
- ❑ Check in with the bridal party for any last-minute changes.

The day before the shower:
- ❑ Make sure all food preparations are ready.
- ❑ Assemble any paraphernalia you will need for the activities.
- ❑ Wrap prizes or gifts you will be awarding.
- ❑ Prepare camera and film.

The Guest List

If you are planning the shower in consultation with the couple of honor, you may organize the guest list by discussing it with the bride and/or groom. If you are planning a surprise shower, you will find that the mother of the bride is usually happy to furnish a list of names, addresses, and phone numbers for family and friends. Be sure to ask each mother if there is anyone she wants included on the guest list.

Financial or logistical limitations may keep some showers small; for others, anyone who knows the bride and groom well and will be invited to the wedding is a potential guest.

Be sure to allow yourself some extra invitations for anyone you may omit by accident.

GUEST LIST

Mailed Invitation	Name	Address
❑	_____	_____
		_____
❑	_____	_____
		_____
❑	_____	_____
		_____
❑	_____	_____
		_____
❑	_____	_____
		_____

GUEST LIST

Mailed Invitation	Name	Address
❑	_____	_____
❑	_____	_____
❑	_____	_____
❑	_____	_____
❑	_____	_____

GUEST LIST

Mailed Invitation	Name	Address
❑	_____	_____
		_____
❑	_____	_____
		_____
❑	_____	_____
		_____
❑	_____	_____
		_____
❑	_____	_____
		_____

GUEST LIST

Mailed Invitation	Name	Address
❏	_____	_____
		_____
❏	_____	_____
		_____
❏	_____	_____
		_____
❏	_____	_____
		_____
❏	_____	_____
		_____

GUEST LIST

Mailed Invitation	Name	Address
❑	_____	_____
		_____
❑	_____	_____
		_____
❑	_____	_____
		_____
❑	_____	_____
		_____
❑	_____	_____
		_____

GUEST LIST

Mailed Invitation	Name	Address
❏	_____	_____
❏	_____	_____
❏	_____	_____
❏	_____	_____
❏	_____	_____

GUEST LIST

Mailed Invitation	Name	Address
❑	_____	_____
		_____
❑	_____	_____
		_____
❑	_____	_____
		_____
❑	_____	_____
		_____
❑	_____	_____
		_____

GUEST LIST

Mailed Invitation	Name	Address
❑	_____	_____
		_____
❑	_____	_____
		_____
❑	_____	_____
		_____
❑	_____	_____
		_____
❑	_____	_____
		_____

GUEST LIST

Mailed Invitation	Name	Address
❑	_____	_____
		_____
❑	_____	_____
		_____
❑	_____	_____
		_____
❑	_____	_____
		_____
❑	_____	_____
		_____

GUEST LIST

Mailed Invitation	Name	Address
❑	_____	_____
		_____
❑	_____	_____
		_____
❑	_____	_____
		_____
❑	_____	_____
		_____
❑	_____	_____
		_____

GUEST LIST

Mailed Invitation	Name	Address
❏	_____	_____
		_____
❏	_____	_____
		_____
❏	_____	_____
		_____
❏	_____	_____
		_____
❏	_____	_____
		_____

GUEST LIST

Mailed Invitation	Name	Address
❑	_____	_____
		_____
❑	_____	_____
		_____
❑	_____	_____
		_____
❑	_____	_____
		_____
❑	_____	_____
		_____

GUEST LIST

Mailed Invitation	Name	Address
❏	_____	_____
		_____
❏	_____	_____
		_____
❏	_____	_____
		_____
❏	_____	_____
		_____
❏	_____	_____
		_____

Guest List

Mailed Invitation	Name	Address
❑	_____	_____
❑	_____	_____
❑	_____	_____
❑	_____	_____
❑	_____	_____

Invitations

☞Invitations

An invitation should grab the attention of the guests. It should create the atmosphere of the shower, letting the invitee know whether the dress code will be formal or outrageous, casual or high camp.

Invitations should contain the following information:

- *Whom the shower is for (guest of honor)*
- *Purpose of the shower (bridal)*
- *Time*
- *Place*
- *Date*
- *At which store(s) bride is registered at*
- *Who is hosting the shower*
- *R.S.V.P. (sometimes "regrets only" are sufficient)*

If the bride is not registered, that line is naturally omitted. Include directions from major roads to the location of the shower. Invitations are usually mailed at least three weeks in advance of the shower date to allow the guests time to arrange their schedules and shop for a gift.

MAKING INVITATIONS

Your first step should be to buy envelopes; you will design the invitations to fit. The most popular envelopes are the 4½" by 5½" size, and are available at most stationery and department stores. Many shops carry color-coordinated envelopes and paper, so you can mix and match or use a color scheme that fits the theme chosen for the shower.

If you're lucky enough to have a computer with the proper software, you can design invitations in that way. Remember, when creating your own invitations, to include all of the pertinent information discussed a few pages earlier in this book.

Always make more invitations than the number of guests you anticipate.

Be sure to double-check all the information on the invitations for accuracy. A wrong address or phone number could be disastrous!

FOLDED NOTES

Copy or trace your chosen card design on one quarter of an 8½-by-11-inch sheet of paper. Then fill in the information on the quarter across from it (see diagram). When you fold the paper, you'll have a card with a design on the front and information inside.

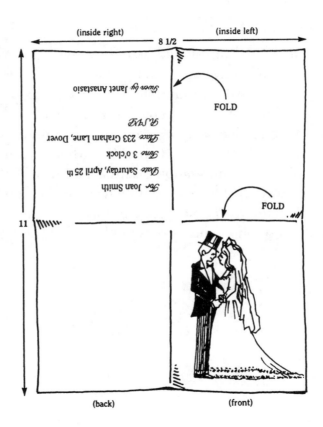

Single-sided Note Card

Here are two examples of single-sided note cards with designs on the front.

Note that one of the designs features the information about the shower on the front of the card.

Bridal Shower

For Joan Smith
Saturday, April 25th
233 Graham Lane, Dover
Three o'clock

RSVP

R.S.V.P.

Respondez s'il vous plait.

R.S.V.P. means "Respond if it pleases you," or, in other words, "Let me know if you will be coming to the shower." Even with this request, people often neglect to respond, and it may be necessary to follow up by calling the guests. When guests R.S.V.P., they will sometimes ask what gifts the new couple needs. If the bride has registered at a department or specialty store, the bridal registry will furnish a guest with a list of the bride's choice in china, linen, crystal, color schemes, and so on. Nevertheless, you should be prepared to have a list of potential gifts to suggest to guests; check each suggestion off when you mention it to a guest. This is not foolproof, but it helps reduce the possibility of duplicate gifts.

Always plan on more people showing up at the party than respond to your invitations!

Shower Location

The shower's setting will become the backdrop of the event; be sure it creates the atmosphere you want. By analyzing what different locations have to offer, you can establish guidelines that will help as you evaluate alternatives. If your budget allows for a location other than someone's living room (which is perfectly acceptable), you may wish to consider some alternatives. The following list may help to point you in the right direction.

- Park
- Public garden
- Clubhouse (i.e., golf, dog track, horse track)
- Halls (i.e., VFW, American Legion, Knights of Columbus)
- Apartment complex (party room)
- Yacht club
- Restaurant
- Museum

If you choose an outdoor location, be prepared for inclement weather; keep a shelter in mind. Remember that indoor space may be limited in some locations.

Children

If you're planning to invite young guests to the shower, you may want to provide some toys, books, or activities especially for the young children. Playing bingo for small prizes (such as crayons and coloring books) is always a popular activity with the young—and the young at heart. Making the food fun is another good idea: Shirley Temples, fruit shakes, hot dogs, and hamburgers are a few ideas you can add to the menu. You might also consider setting up a separate table or play area for the children to play in.

To Open the Shower...

Perhaps you are looking for the best way to get the shower started. Why not consider beginning the shower by reading one of the following memorable quotes on love and marriage to the assembly?

To be loved, be lovable.
—OVID

When two people are at one in their inmost hearts,
they shatter even the strength of iron or of bronze.
—I CHING

Love and you shall be loved.
—RALPH WALDO EMERSON

Love sought is good, but given unsought is better.
—WILLIAM SHAKESPEARE

To love for the sake of being loved is human,
but to love for the sake of loving is angelic.
—ALPHONSE MARIE LOUIS DE LAMARTINE

Love is all you need.
—JOHN LENNON & PAUL McCARTNEY

Marriage is that relation between a man and woman in which the independence is equal, the dependence mutual, and the obligation reciprocal.
—L. K. ANSPACHER

The supreme happiness of life is the conviction of being loved for yourself, or more correctly, being loved in spite of yourself.
—VICTOR HUGO

Between Hope and Fear, Love makes her home.
—RAMON LULLY

O, human love! thou spirit given On Earth, of all we hope in Heaven!
—EDGAR ALLAN POE

Love is the emblem of eternity.
—MME DE STAËL

There is no remedy for love but to love more.
—HENRY DAVID THOREAU

Love is not getting, but giving;
It is goodness, and humor, and peace and pure living.
—HENRY VAN DYKE

Keep thy eyes wide open before marriage, and half shut afterwards.
—BENJAMIN FRANKLIN

Love comforteth like sunshine after rain.
—WILLIAM SHAKESPEARE

Love begets love.
—THEODORE ROETHKE

Perdition catch my soul but I do love thee!
And when I love thee not, chaos is come again.
—WILLIAM SHAKESPEARE

Love, all alike, no season knows, nor clime,
Nor hours, days, months, which are the rags of time.
—JOHN DONNE

Give all to love; obey thy heart.
—RALPH WALDO EMERSON

Hail wedded love, mysterious law, true source of humanity.
—JOHN MILTON

I wonder by my troth, what thou and I did till we lov'd?
—JOHN DONNE

Theme Showers

Theme Showers

Theme showers have become increasingly popular in recent years. These are parties with an overriding element that makes gift selection easier for the guest. The theme, which can be built around anything the newlyweds could use, should be specified on the invitation.

There are any number of variations; try to encourage family and friends to be creative in coming up with ideas. A strong theme can turn a humdrum affair into a fast-moving, fun-filled party.

On the following pages, you will find some theme ideas to help point you in the right direction. Before you make your final decision, take into consideration the location of the shower and the time of year it is being held. Following is a list of suggested shower themes.

Relative Shower   *Money Tree Shower*
Domestic or Pantry Shower   *No-Expense Shower*
Champagne and Wine Shower   *Moving Away Shower*
Barbecue Shower   *Honeymoon Shower*
Special Time Shower   *Lingerie/Personal Shower*
Pamper the Bride Shower   *Tea Party*
Basket Shower   *Traditional Bridal/Wedding Shower*
Bedroom and Bathroom Shower   *Around-the-World Shower*

RELATIVE SHOWER

This kind of shower is for relatives of the bride and groom only, though you could also include the non-family members of the wedding party. Ask each family member to bring a would-be heirloom or treasured gift from the family's past that was handed down or could be handed down. Such items as hand-crocheted doilies, lace tablecloths, bedspreads, china, crystal, old family recipes, and albums with baby pictures of the bride and groom are all appropriate gifts.

You can turn this shower into a family hour by asking each guest to share the story of the memento—where it came from, how old it is, and so on. The possibilities are endless!

DOMESTIC OR PANTRY SHOWER

This is the most popular theme, because of the wide variety of items a newly married couple needs. Gifts can range from brooms, mops, cookware, kitchen witches, towels, oven mitts, and kitchen clocks to canned goods and spices for stocking the pantry shelves. A domestic shower is probably the least glamorous of all the showers, but given today's economy, even modest gifts like salt and pepper shakers are appreciated!

Encourage the guests to be creative in wrapping the gifts. Perhaps a wooden spoon could be wrapped in a new dishtowel! You might even ask each guest to bring one of his or her favorite recipes along and tell everyone where it originated and how he or she came by it.

CHAMPAGNE AND WINE SHOWER

Keep in mind that this works well only if the guest list is small (around ten people). Each guest is asked to bring a nice bottle of wine or champagne. You can keep your menu very simple, but the decor should be elegant. Use long-stemmed champagne glasses and ask guests to dress up. Set as elaborate a table as possible: white cotton or linen tablecloth with matching napkins, silver, and crystal. You can even put long-stemmed roses in a crystal vase as a centerpiece. Make sure the champagne is iced properly, and delegate someone (perhaps the groom) to open the champagne so the host won't have to struggle with the bottle during the shower.

Provide sparkling apple juice or soft drinks for any guests who prefer not to drink alcohol. Take into consideration the ages of the guests, and be sure no one over-indulges before driving.

BARBECUE SHOWER

For a spring or summer wedding, a barbecue shower may be the perfect thing. This kind of shower also goes over well as a co-ed shower, or for couples who have been living together and already have most of the classic "domestic" shower gifts. Guests have a large variety of gifts to choose from, such as picnic baskets, barbecue utensils, lounge chairs, and croquet sets. A good group gift—such as a grill—can be a big hit.

You might even be able to include a quick game of volleyball or softball!

(*Helpful hint:* Outdoor locations, such as parks or beaches, are the best settings for this theme shower.)

SPECIAL TIME SHOWER

For this theme, give each guest a specific time of day and ask him or her to bring a gift used at that time. For example, three A.M. would tend to suggest sheets, while six A.M. could be an alarm clock. Alternatively, you can assign different months with instructions to bring a gift appropriate to that time of year. For instance, December suggests the holidays. The guest could bring decorations such as tree lights, a floral wreath for the front door, wrapping paper, or even greeting cards.

You can build a shower theme around any holiday; your guests will love it.

Pamper the Bride Shower

Guests are instructed to bring gifts for the bride to pamper herself with. A gift certificate for a massage or a whirlpool, for example, a bottle of fine perfume, or a bottle of champagne might be appropriate. One useful gift your guest-of-honor would probably love for wedding pampering would be a manicure or a facial. These kinds of gifts are much-appreciated indulgences that can lessen the stress of an impending wedding.

BASKET SHOWER

A basket shower allows your guests to be creative in their gift selections. Inform them that the gift can come in a basket—or can even *be* a basket. Such items as covered casserole dishes with a basket server, a hand-painted basket, a wicker wastebasket, and a basket filled with guest towels and decorative soaps and oils are all possibilities. You can even choose a wicker laundry basket or hamper!

This theme will allow you to use colored baskets as theme decorations: perhaps baskets with flowers in them as centerpieces that can be given away as prizes.

BEDROOM AND BATHROOM SHOWER

Actually, this type of shower can be for any room in the house, but it seems to work best with the bed and bath theme. Assign guests one room or the other.

Necessities like sheets, blankets, and comforters are always needed and appreciated, but so are clock radios, paintings, bedroom lamps, shower curtains, and other accessories. Monogrammed towels coordinated with throw rugs, a scale, and bathroom accessories make good bathroom gifts.

This type of shower could win the newly married couple a full-page spread in *Good Housekeeping*!

MONEY TREE SHOWER

This is one shower that provides couples with a gift they won't return! Most young couples just starting out are not quite sure of the kinds of furnishings or accessories they'll need. A cash gift, tactfully offered in a money-holder or card, is often the most helpful present.

You can use any kind of decorated potted tree (perhaps with twinkling lights) to display the envelopes. As the guests arrive, they attach their gift of money to the branches of the tree with clothespins or colored ribbons. Other ideas: Use a tree branch in a large vase (if you'd rather not purchase a live tree), or make a poster with a drawing of a tree and pin or tape the envelopes to it.

No-Expense Shower

When the bride-to-be has had several showers and you would still like to have a party but are afraid the guests will feel a financial pinch, this is the way to go. Just ask for gifts that won't cost anything—recipes, for instance. Ask each guest to contribute a favorite recipe, written or typed on a three-by-five-inch index card and enclosed in a greeting card. If guests design their own cards, the party will be even more fun. As the guest of honor opens each card, file it in an indexed recipe file. At the end of the party, give the box of recipes to the bride-to-be.

Another option for a no-expense shower is the idea book party. Ask each guest to write out a time-saving household idea or a cleaning trick he or she has learned over the years. Combine the ideas in a notebook or scrapbook and present it to the bride-to-be at the end of the party.

Moving Away Shower

The decorations for this theme party could include maps and posters of the place where the couple will be living. Post farewell signs on the wall. Suggest that the guests keep the gifts small and packable: first aid kit, change-of-address cards, subscription to a hometown newspaper, tourist materials, or a photo album with pictures of old friends. If the couple is traveling by car, they may appreciate an emergency tire inflater, warning flares, or a flashlight with extra batteries. There are many other useful gifts that can help the couple with their relocation.

Honeymoon Shower

If you know the couple's honeymoon destination ahead of time, you may want to consider this kind of shower. Decorations could include travel posters and brochures describing the couple's destination. If the couple does not already have one, a good camera with a supply of film can make a great group gift. Another group gift possibility is to call ahead to arrange for an intimate dinner at the hotel or inn where the couple will be staying, or have a bottle of champagne or a fruit basket sent to their room.

For couples who do not plan on going away for a honeymoon, this party can be a real treat. Gifts can include laundry service, maid service, gift certificates to restaurants, theater or concert tickets, a massage for two, tapes of romantic music, or even a weekend at a nice hotel.

LINGERIE/PERSONAL SHOWER

Traditionally this is for the bride only, but since it's more common for the groom to attend the shower these days, it could be fun to include some special gifts for him as well. Nightgowns or personal lingerie are gifts a bride can take on her honeymoon, but don't forget the groom can also use personal grooming items such as shaving lotion, razors, and scented soap. On the romantic side, silk boxer shorts might be a nice gift choice for the groom.

TEA PARTY

An afternoon tea is still a favorite way to entertain guests. Presentation can range from a very elaborate setting at a dining-room table to a simple round table in a corner of the living room. The tradition is to serve something hot, something cold, and some sweets. Plan on at least three or four goodies per person. Better to have too much than too little!

To perk up any brand of tea, serve it with sticks of cinnamon; slices of lime, lemon, or oranges; or a sprig of fresh mint. In the summer, tall glasses of mint-topped iced tea—or hot tea—could be served. To avoid traffic jams at the table, pass the refreshments around after the guests have their tea and are seated. Some favorite goodies for tea parties include:

- Hot buttered muffins
- Nut bread
- Pound cake (sliced thin)
- Buttered biscuits
- Butter sandwiches

Gift ideas for this shower would include china tea cups and dessert plates, a sterling silver creamer and sugar bowl, or a china tea pot.

TRADITIONAL BRIDAL/WEDDING SHOWER

Despite all the variations, traditional bridal showers are still popular, even if the gifts given today are a bit different than those of years past. The bridal shower our mothers and grandmothers had was a women-only affair where the bride received all sorts of practical presents, mainly kitchen and various other household items. In years past, the rationale behind this "women only" party was that maintaining the household was the bride's primary responsibility—and she would need all the good wishes and help she could get. It was customary for a wishing well to be placed near the guest of honor's seat; when the guests came in, they would place small gifts or gadgets such as wooden spoons, bottle openers, and any kind of grab gift into the wishing well. Today, with women rarely able to devote themselves to homemaking full time, shower themes have changed considerably, but you could still pay homage to the past by having a traditional, time-honored shower that features a wishing well.

AROUND-THE-WORLD SHOWER

Our country has always been a melting pot of numerous cultures. An around-the-world shower is a great way to emphasize the varied heritages of your guests.

Each guest brings a gift that represents some aspect of his or her ethnic background. A guest with an Irish grandparent, for instance, might bring a bottle of Bailey's Irish Creme liqueur for the bride and groom. Someone of Ukranian descent might bring a Ukranian Easter egg set.

If most or all the people on the guest list are predominantly of a single ethnic background, have each guest pick a nation to represent with a gift. Alternatively, you could select a single nation for all guests—say, France—and have each person bring a gift that somehow connects to that nation.

OTHER SHOWER IDEAS

Here are a few more theme shower ideas to consider.

Gadget Shower
Possible gift ideas: Egg slicer, pepper mill, apple slicer/corer, food chopper, melon baller.

Plastic Shower
Possible gift ideas: Pail, soap dish, spatulas, pitchers, dish pan, tupper ware.

China and Glass Shower
Possible gift ideas: Decanter, candy dish, sugar bowl, cream pitcher, vase.

Closet Shower
Possible gift ideas: Garment bags, hat boxes, slacks hangers, shoe tree, floor or wall shoe rack, cedar spray, scented hangers.

Fix-it Shower
Possible gift ideas: Hand saw, hammer, machine oil, masking tape, heavy-duty stapler, electric screw drivers.

Decorations

Decorations

Party decorating can be fun; simple decorations like colorful balloons or balloon bouquets, flowers, crepe paper streamers, or paper bells help make a festive party. You'll want to make the shower area stand out and be noticed right from the start. Some themes suggest their own decorating ideas; others require some imagination.

The cost of running a shower adds up fast. Cutting costs, however, does not mean losing the party atmosphere. The "budget" shower can still be simple, elaborate, traditional, or unique. If your party space is less than ideal, you may have to do something radical. First, decide on the color scheme. Then view the room objectively, keeping your color choices in mind. Use your imagination; base your decorating on what is necessary to transform the area into the look you desire. Review the theme and color selections of your shower once again with decorations in mind.

Bringing the Room to Life

There are so many ways to help make any room or hall come alive. Some rental halls are rather dreary, with old lighting fixtures and ungainly poles in awkward places throughout the room. The poles can easily be decorated with bows and crepe paper. If the existing light fixtures are too hideous to display in the open (and many are), cover them with inexpensive decorations; white umbrellas or parasols will hide old fixtures well. Simply cut off the parasol handle, fasten pretty ribbons (in your color scheme) at the tips of the parasol, and tie the parasol directly below the fixture. Then decorate with more streamers, flowers, bows, and ribbons.

Hang a paper parasol above the guest of honor's chair. These can be purchased from a paper products store.

Ceiling banners can add a lot to a drab hall. They don't have to be made of fabric; they can be made from butcher's paper or tissue paper glued to create patterns. You can create the banners to match the wedding colors. For a delicate version of a banner, use wide lengths of netting or cheesecloth and attach paper or silk flowers decorated with ribbons and streamers.

If you have a computer or know someone who does, Banner Mania is a great software program for any kind of party or gathering. You can create all kinds of banners to pass along good wishes to the bridal pair.

Scents help make a room inviting while adding a feeling of intimacy to a party space. You can have fresh flowers on the tables—gardenias, roses, narcissuses, or freesia work well. The same effect can be achieved by placing scented candles or fragrant potpourri around the room. Cinnamon sticks and cloves placed around the food table are also a nice touch. Wicker baskets used as centerpieces and filled with fresh bread or rolls, flowers, fresh fruit, or silk flowers add festivity to the room.

Making Tissue Flowers

1. Cut strips of tissue about seven inches long and three inches wide, and accordion-fold them together using two contrasting colors. Trim a petal shape on one end.

2. Open the packet outward and begin rolling and gathering the paper to form a flower. Gently fan the petals for fullness. Tape the bottom of the flower to keep it together. These can be used to decorate chairs and tables, and as centerpieces.

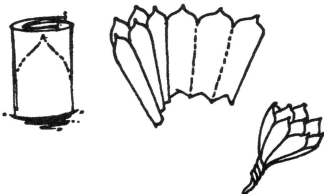

ᴄ Favors

Giving favors is an act of kindness and a thank-you to the guests, all in one. You can add a special touch to a party by preparing a number of small gifts or decorative items for your guests. These can be used to decorate the table as well. You can buy small gift items as favors or be creative and make them yourself.

Following are some suggestions for home-made favors:

- *Wooden Spoons*
- *Potpourri Hearts*
- *Potpourri Ball Ornament*

WOODEN SPOONS

These come in many sizes. You will need:

A roll of netting, any color
Colored almonds or mints
Ribbon

Cut the net into squares, place the candy into the center, pull up the four corners and tie the ribbon into a bow around the wooden spoon.

POTPOURRI HEARTS

Get as much lace as needed to have a favor for each guest. Cut it into any size you want. Use a heart-shaped pattern to cut out the lace hearts.

Place one piece on top of another. Hand- or machine-sew the two pieces of lace together, after you have put a generous amount of potpourri into the center of both pieces. Put a bow on the top with a loop to hang it.

Guests can hang these in drawers or closets, or place them in any room as a freshener.

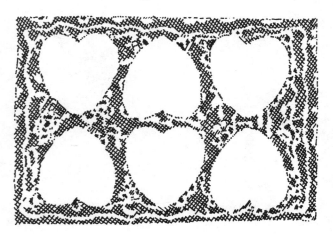

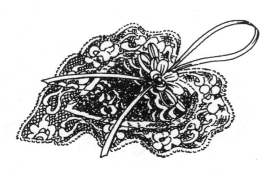

POTPOURRI BALL ORNAMENT

These can be made in various color schemes to match the theme of your shower. Materials you will need for each favor:

One clear plastic tree ornament (make sure the top is removable)
1/2 yard ribbon (of your choice) for the top of ornament
1/2 yard lace trim
small silk or dried flowers
1 small bag of colorful potpourri
glue gun

First remove the top of the ornament. Pour the potpourri through the top until full and replace the top. Glue the lace trim around the top of the ball—you may choose to glue on several layers. From here on it's your party. You can be as creative as you wish.

⚘Corsage

Every bride-to-be loves to receive a corsage!

Usually, a corsage made from real flowers is presented to the guest of honor, but you may choose to order a silk corsage from a store. This kind of corsage can be easier to store and more long-lasting. Match the color scheme of the shower. Present the corsage to the guest of honor after she has been seated.

Be sure to order the corsage at least one or two weeks before the shower.

(*Hint:* See if it is possible to find out ahead of time what the bride will be wearing on the day of shower; this way the corsage can be tailored to coordinate with her outfit.)

Keepsake Rehearsal Bouquet

The bride may want to create a keepsake bouquet to be used at the rehearsal as a substitute for her real bouquet. Gather all the ribbons and bows from the presents at the shower. Get a white or colored paper plate and poke several holes in it. Stick the bows on the paper plate, pull the ribbons through the holes and arrange them in the form of a bouquet. Try to gather enough ribbons to have a handful to hold securely.

Games

Games

Guests should sense a warm and friendly ambiance before the bride arrives—and the games that follow will help you to set the perfect mood. The diversions included here are only a small sampling of the trivia games, quizzes, or guessing games you may wish to initiate. *Hint*: Any game played with the anticipation of winning a prize will encourage the guests to be participants rather than observers. In addition, playing party games and winning surprise gifts is a nice way for all of the guests to become better acquainted.

Best Guess

Fill a large decorative jar with white or colored almonds. Ask the guests to try to figure out how many almonds are in the jar and write their answers on a piece of paper. They can take as long as they want to come up with a number. The game concludes at the end of the shower, when you announce the number of almonds in the jar and when you award a prize—the jar and the almonds—to the person whose guess was closest.

SCRAMBLED LETTERS

Use words associated with love and marriage, such as the word kiss (siks), love (voel), garter (tergar), and the names of the bride and groom. This list can go on and on. Set a time limit; award a prize to the guest with the most correct solutions.

MYSTERY SPICES

Find ten jars of different spices. Place masking tape over the labels to cover the type of spice that is in each jar. Spread them out on a table and let the guests try to guess which spice is in each jar. Players may pick up and examine the jars. Set a time limit; the guest with the most correct answers wins. This is not as easy as it sounds—many spices look alike. When the game is over, give the spices to the guest of honor (not the winner).

BRIDE'S CHATTER

During the shower, inconspicuously keep a journal of all the bride's comments as she opens the presents. After she is through opening all of her gifts, read all of the comments out loud to the group for a good laugh. You may also choose to record the shower on tape and give it to the bride as a parting gift.

FAMOUS COUPLE TRIVIA

In recent years trivia games have become a favorite pastime for adults and children alike.

Following are a few examples of some trivia questions you might use to test your guests' memories. Warning: they get more difficult as you go along!

1. What famous singing TV couple of the '60s and '70s eventually had their own TV show? (Hint: they had a daughter named Chastity.)

2. What was the maiden name of Prince Andrew's wife?

3. What was Roy Rogers' wife's name?

4. What are the names of Lucy and Ricky Ricardo's best friends on *I Love Lucy*?

5. What famous couple were mom and dad to David and Rick?

6. Who was Alice's boyfriend on *The Brady Bunch*? What did he do?

7. What cartoon couple was played by Shelley Duvall and Robin Williams in a big-budget film?

8. What prince married Queen Victoria of England in 1840?

9. Of whom did Spencer Tracy say, "There's not much meat on her, but what's there is cherce"?

10. Name the legendary married acting duo who appeared together in *Cocoon*.

11. Who was Odysseus's wife?

12. She was a playwright and memoirist; he wrote some of the world's most popular mysteries. Name the couple.

13. He was one of the leading English Romantic poets; she wrote the classic gothic novel *Frankenstein*. Name the couple.

14. He won (and refused) the 1964 Nobel Prize for Literature; she wrote *The Second Sex*. Name this famous couple.

15. Together, this couple wrote the script for one of the most beloved movie musicals, *Singin' in the Rain*. Name them.

ANSWERS (Upside down so you won't peek!)

15. Betty Comden and Adolph Green
14. Jean-Paul Sartre and Simone de Beauvoir
13. Percy Bysshe Shelley and Mary Wollstonecraft Shelley
12. Lillian Hellman and Dashiell Hammett
11. Penelope
10. Hume Cronyn and Jessica Tandy
9. Katharine Hepburn
8. Prince Albert
7. Olive Oyl and Popeye
6. Sam; he was a butcher
5. Ozzie and Harriet Nelson
4. Fred and Ethel Mertz
3. Dale Evans
2. Lady Sarah Ferguson
1. Sonny and Cher

MEMORY GAME

After the bride-to-be has opened all of her gifts, ask her to leave the room for a few minutes. (Explain this activity to her in advance, so she knows what to expect.) Once she has left the room, pass out paper and pens and ask the guests what the guest of honor is wearing. What color are her shoes? What color is her nail polish? What color is her dress? Does she have earrings on? The questions should address every visible article of clothing. The guest who comes up with the most correct answers is the winner.

ANNIVERSARY DOOR PRIZE

Ask all of your guests for the date of their wedding anniversary. Unmarried guests may use their birthdays. Whoever has an anniversary or birthday closest to the wedding date wins a prize—perhaps a calendar or planner. This is a great deal of fun for everyone!

☙Prizes

When choosing prizes, try to make them useful as well as unique. If your budget allows, spend a little more on a few nicer prizes, rather than many inexpensive ones; keep your guest list in mind when selecting items.

It doesn't hurt to have a few extra prizes in case of ties. Here are a few basic shower prizes you can keep on hand at little extra cost.

Shopping list pads *Note cards or stationery*
Mugs *Candy*
Bubble bath *Magnets*
Coasters *Fancy recipe cards*
Fancy soaps *Hand lotion*
Cocktail napkins *Unusual pens*
Mixed nuts

If there happens to be more than one winner for a game, and only one prize, the hostess should pick a number between one and one hundred. The person who guesses closest to the correct number is the winner.

↜Cake Ideas

Cakes can be made in any shape or size. Once you have chosen the theme of the shower, you can begin to think of a shower cake design. Keeping in mind the time of year the wedding will be held in and the couple's lifestyle, design the cake with appropriate colors. Any holiday occurring near the date of the shower, for instance, will probably yield some interesting design ideas.

On the following pages are some examples of cake designs you may want to consider using.

Heart-shaped

Umbrella

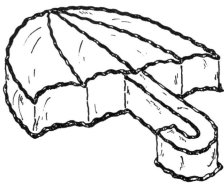

Basket full of best wishes   **Sheet cake in shape of a gift package**

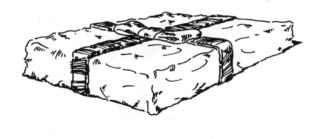

Sheet cake decorated
to match the invitation

Bible cake

Culinary Choices

Hiring a Caterer

Caterers can help make choices with food, settings, and centerpieces, and can provide many helpful ideas for the shower.

Some caterers will handle the whole shower—food, flowers, decorations, even music. Whether to select a full-service caterer is up to your budget and preference.

There is a middle-of-the-road alternative to a caterer, and it is less expensive. A new kind of professional, called the party planner, functions as a time-saving organizer who will scout locations, come up with theme or decor ideas, and hire the best people to take care of food, flowers, decorations, and entertainment. The planner can relieve a lot of the pressure of organizing a shower. Your budget and experience will help you make the right choices.

If any of your guests have special dietary restrictions or mobility problems or any special needs, it is wise to determine what these are and have the caterer or planner prepare for them in advance.

ᴄAppetizers

Serving appetizers to the guests before the bride-to-be arrives can help make the waiting a little easier for everyone. Small finger foods, such as stuffed mushrooms, chicken wings, meatballs, or calzones will be a big hit at any shower.

Following is a list of suggested appetizer recipes.

Calzone (Rolled Pizza)   *Beef Teriyaki Strips*
Fried Chicken Wings   *Shrimp Cocktail*
Stuffed Mushrooms   *Scallops*
Crab Cakes   *Chicken Fingers*
Zucchini Appetizers   *Vegetable Platter*
Meat Balls

CALZONE (ROLLED PIZZA)

1 loaf frozen bread dough or pizza dough
8 oz. shredded mozzarella cheese
4 slices capacola
1/4 cup grated Parmesan cheese

4 slices Genoa salami
4 slices mortadella
4 slices ham
(all meats thinly sliced)

Thaw dough and let it rise until doubled. Divide in half. Roll out to about 12" x 12". Put filling on dough (meat, then cheese); sprinkle lightly with oil. Roll jelly-roll fashion, pinch ends, then bake until golden brown at 400°F for 20 minutes. Remove from oven and slice. Italian sausages (cooked) may also be used, as can peppers, onions, and mushrooms. Meat should be chopped in small pieces.

FRIED CHICKEN WINGS

10 lbs. chicken wings
4 tbsp. soy sauce
1 whole garlic bud (crushed)

1 tbsp. salt
2 tbsp. sugar
chopped ginger root or powdered ginger

Separate tips from joints. Marinate wings for 24 hours, then deep fry until golden brown.

STUFFED MUSHROOMS

35 large mushrooms
2 sticks butter (8 oz.)
$1/2$ tsp. garlic salt
salt to taste

1 onion, finely chopped
1 cup chicken bouillon
$1/2$ package stuffing mix (seasoned)
pepper to taste

Clean mushrooms. Remove and chop stems. In $1/2$ cup butter, sauté chopped stems and onion until onions look clear. Add $1/2$ package prepared stuffing mix, 1 cup chicken bouillon, and salt and pepper to taste. Add $1/2$ tsp. garlic salt. Stuff caps with mixture. In a 10" x 15" pan, melt $1/2$ cup butter, place mushrooms in the pan. Bake at 350°F for 15 minutes. Then broil 3 to 5 minutes. To freeze, bake only 10 minutes and let cool, then cover with foil and place in freezer. To serve, bake unthawed for 15 minutes, then broil.

CRAB CAKES

Combine one 7$\frac{1}{2}$ ounce can of crabmeat (remove any bony bits) with:

$\frac{1}{2}$ cup finely chopped celery
$\frac{1}{2}$ cup seasoned bread crumbs
1 tbsp. lemon juice
dash of pepper

1 small onion (finely chopped)
1 egg (beaten)
1 tbsp. chopped parsley

Form into small round cakes (2" diameter by $\frac{1}{2}$" thick) with your hands. Fry in oil until golden brown on all sides.

Zucchini Appetizers

3 cups thinly sliced zucchini (4 small)
1/2 cup finely chopped onion
1/2 cup vegetable oil
1/2 tsp. salt
1/2 tsp. oregano
1 clove of garlic (finely chopped)

1 cup biscuit/pancake mix
1/2 cup grated Parmesan cheese
2 tbsp. snipped parsley
1/2 tsp. seasoned salt
dash of pepper
4 eggs (slightly beaten)

Heat oven to 350°F, grease oblong pan (13" x 9" x 2"). Mix all ingredients; spread in pan. Bake until golden brown, about 25 minutes. Cut into pieces about 2" x 1". Makes about 4 dozen appetizers.

MEAT BALLS

1 lb. ground beef
½ cup grated cheese
½ clove garlic (minced)
1 tsp. salt

2 eggs (beaten)
2 tbsp. chopped parsley
1 tsp. crushed oregano
dash of pepper

Combine ingredients, mixing well. Form into small balls (makes about 20). Brown in a frying pan with 2 to 3 tbsp. of olive oil.

BEEF TERIYAKI STRIPS

1 to 2 lbs. sirloin strips or beef roast cut in thin strips.

Marinade sauce:

1 cup water
1 crushed beef bouillon cube
1 tsp. garlic (minced)
2 tbsp. lemon juice

$1/2$ cup soy sauce
$1/4$ cup brown sugar
1 small onion (finely chopped)
2 tbsp. olive oil

Mix all ingredients for sauce together in a deep bowl. Place the strips in the sauce and let them marinate for 6 hours. Broil the tips for 10 to 15 minutes. (May also be cooked to taste on a grill.)

SHRIMP COCKTAIL

Shell fresh cooked shrimp (remove any veins). Chill the shrimp at least one hour and place on a bed of dried lettuce or in lettuce-lined cocktail cups. Serve plain or with prepared cocktail sauce.

(*Serving Suggestion*: Arranging chilled shrimp on a large platter surrounding a decorative crystal or·glass bowl filled with cocktail sauce adds a touch of elegance to any table.)

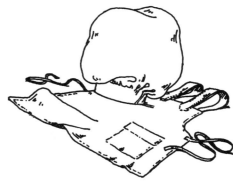

SCALLOPS

Marinate in a lemon-butter sauce:

1 lb. small bay scallops
1/2 tsp. salt
1/4 cup lemon juice

1/3 cup butter or margarine (melted)
dash pepper
2 tbsp. minced parsley

Heat oven to 350°F. Combine ingredients in a casserole dish, sprinkle with seasoned bread crumbs, and bake for 15 to 20 minutes. Serve warm; toothpicks may be used as utensils.

VEGETABLE PLATTER

1 head raw broccoli (cut in small pieces)
2 cucumbers (sliced into thin, long strips)

16 oz. raw carrots (sliced)
1 zucchini (sliced into thin, long strips)

Place vegetables around a platter or a round dish. Serve with a sour cream and dry onion soup mix dip, plain sour cream, cottage cheese, or any of your favorite dips.

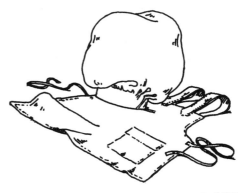

CHICKEN FINGERS

1 to 2 lbs. boneless, skinned chicken pieces 1 egg (beaten)
½ cup milk 1 cup seasoned bread crumbs

Slice the chicken into thin strips. Combine milk and egg. Soak the chicken strips in the milk and egg mixture. Remove strips and roll over bread crumbs until completely covered. Fry in a pan with 2 tbsp. of olive oil until golden brown.

⌒Desserts

Don't skip dessert! This is a break in the shower most guests look forward to, when they can have a sweet with coffee, tea, or milk. Dessert also signifies a time to relax for everyone—including the guest of honor and the host.

Following are a variety of popular dessert recipes.

Frosted Pumpkin Bars
Favorite Brownies
Dutch Apple Cake

Pistachio Surprise Bars
Raspberry Squares

FROSTED PUMPKIN BARS

Pumpkin Bar ingredients:

4 eggs
1 cup oil
2 cups flour
2 tsp. cinnamon
1 tsp. baking soda

$1^2/_3$ cups sugar
1 15-oz. can pumpkin or squash
2 tsp. baking powder
1 tsp. salt

Frosting ingredients:

1 8-oz. pkg. cream cheese (softened)
1 tsp. vanilla
$^1/_8$ to $^1/_4$ cup milk

$^1/_2$ cup butter or margarine (softened)
1 16-oz. box confectioner's sugar

Mix well in the order given. Beat at medium speed until smooth. Pour into ungreased 15" x 10" x 1" pan. Bake at 350°F for 25 to 30 minutes. Combine the frosting ingredients; frost when completely cooled.

FAVORITE BROWNIES

8 oz. cream cheese
4 eggs
1 stick butter (4 oz.)
1 cup flour

2 cup sugar
4-oz. pkg. chocolate squares
1 tsp. vanilla
1 cup nuts (optional)

Combine sugar, butter, cream cheese, and beaten eggs. Mix until smooth. Melt chocolate. Add flour and vanilla and fold in nuts. Mix well. Bake at 325°F for 30 minutes in a 9" x 13" pan.

DUTCH APPLE CAKE

2 cups flour
3 tsp. baking powder
$^1/_4$ cup melted shortening
1 cup milk
1 tsp. cinnamon mixed with $^1/_2$ cup sugar

$^1/_2$ tsp. salt
$^1/_3$ cup sugar
1 egg (beaten)
3 apples (thinly sliced)

Sift dry ingredients together. Beat egg, add milk and shortening, and add to sifted dry ingredients. Stir quickly, spread in buttered pan. Arrange apple slices in row over top, pressing them lightly into the dough. Sprinkle with sugar-spice mixture. Dot with butter and bake for about 25 minutes in a 350°F oven. Top with confectioner's sugar; serve warm.

PISTACHIO SURPRISE BARS

1 tsp. salt
1½ cups flour
1 lb. plain M & Ms candies
1½ cups sugar

1 tsp. baking powder
1 pkg. instant pistachio pudding
4 tsp. oil
3 eggs

Mix together salt, baking powder, flour, and pudding mix. Mix together oil, sugar, and eggs. Add dry mix to wet mix. Stir well, add candy. Bake at 350°F in greased 10" x 13" pan for 25 to 35 minutes. Cut while warm.

RASPBERRY SQUARES

3 cups all-purpose flour
1 cup sugar
$1/2$ cup butter (softened)
2 tsp. vanilla

1 tsp. baking powder
$1/2$ cup shortening (softened)
2 eggs (beaten)
1 12-oz. jar raspberry jam

Combine all ingredients except raspberry jam in a large mixing bowl and mix well. Spread $3/4$ of the mix onto an ungreased cookie sheet, pressing with your knuckles. Spread the raspberry jam on top of mix (but do not touch the edges of the pan). Take the rest of the mix and sprinkle in little pieces on top of the jam. Bake for 25 to 30 minutes at 350°F.

After the Shower:
Record of Gifts for Thank-you Notes

Tradition and simple good manners require that the recipient of a gift thank the giver in writing with a note. Without records of who gave which gift at a shower, however, the guests-of-honor will never remember who gave what. They'll find it extremely difficult trying to write thank-you notes to every gift giver expressing their gratitude for that special gift. The charts on the following pages will help the bride keep a record of all the gifts she received and when, and whether she sent her thank-you notes out.

It is common for someone who is involved in throwing the shower (often the maid-of-honor) to fill in the name and gift information while the bride is opening her gifts.

SHOWER RECORD

Theme: _____

Hostess: _____

Date: _____

Place: _____

Guest	Gift	Sent Note
_____	_____	❑
_____	_____	❑
_____	_____	❑
_____	_____	❑
_____	_____	❑
_____	_____	❑

SHOWER RECORD

Theme: _____

Hostess: _____

Date: _____

Place: _____

Guest	Gift	Sent Note
_____	_____	❏
_____	_____	❏
_____	_____	❏
_____	_____	❏
_____	_____	❏
_____	_____	❏

SHOWER RECORD

Theme: _____

Hostess: _____

Date: _____

Place: _____

Guest	Gift	Sent Note
_____	_____	❏
_____	_____	❏
_____	_____	❏
_____	_____	❏
_____	_____	❏
_____	_____	❏

SHOWER RECORD

Theme: _____

Hostess: _____

Date: _____

Place: _____

Guest	**Gift**	**Sent Note**
_____	_____	❏
_____	_____	❏
_____	_____	❏
_____	_____	❏
_____	_____	❏
_____	_____	❏

SHOWER RECORD

Theme: _____

Hostess: _____

Date: _____

Place: _____

Guest	Gift	Sent Note
_____	_____	❑
_____	_____	❑
_____	_____	❑
_____	_____	❑
_____	_____	❑
_____	_____	❑

SHOWER RECORD

Theme: _____

Hostess: _____

Date: _____

Place: _____

Guest	Gift	Sent Note
_____	_____	❑
_____	_____	❑
_____	_____	❑
_____	_____	❑
_____	_____	❑
_____	_____	❑

SHOWER RECORD

Theme: _____

Hostess: _____

Date: _____

Place: _____

Guest	Gift	Sent Note
_____	_____	❏
_____	_____	❏
_____	_____	❏
_____	_____	❏
_____	_____	❏
_____	_____	❏

SHOWER RECORD

Theme: _____

Hostess: _____

Date: _____

Place: _____

Guest	Gift	Sent Note
_____	_____	❑
_____	_____	❑
_____	_____	❑
_____	_____	❑
_____	_____	❑
_____	_____	❑

Shower Record

Theme: _____

Hostess: _____

Date: _____

Place: _____

Guest	Gift	Sent Note
_____	_____	❑
_____	_____	❑
_____	_____	❑
_____	_____	❑
_____	_____	❑
_____	_____	❑

SHOWER RECORD

Theme: _____

Hostess: _____

Date: _____

Place: _____

Guest	Gift	Sent Note
_____	_____	❑
_____	_____	❑
_____	_____	❑
_____	_____	❑
_____	_____	❑
_____	_____	❑

Shower Record

Theme: _____

Hostess: _____

Date: _____

Place: _____

Guest	Gift	Sent Note
_____	_____	❑
_____	_____	❑
_____	_____	❑
_____	_____	❑
_____	_____	❑
_____	_____	❑

The following pages will allow family members and special friends the opportunity to share with the bride-to-be any words of wisdom or secret tips they might have on married life. The bride-to-be will have this record of advice to look back on over the many anniversaries she will celebrate. The many traditions can be passed on for generations.

ADVICE RECORD

Date: _____   **Hostess:** _____

Guest

_____

_____

_____

_____

_____

Advice

_____

_____

_____

_____

_____

_____

_____

_____

ADVICE RECORD

Date: _____   Hostess: _____

Guest

_____

_____

_____

_____

_____

Advice

_____

_____

_____

_____

_____

_____

_____

_____

ADVICE RECORD

Date: _____   Hostess: _____

Guest	Advice

ADVICE RECORD

Date: _____   Hostess: _____

Guest

_____

_____

_____

_____

_____

Advice

_____

_____

_____

_____

_____

_____

_____

_____

_____

ADVICE RECORD

Date: _____   Hostess: _____

Guest

Advice

_____ _____

_____ _____

_____ _____

_____ _____

_____ _____

_____ _____

_____ _____

130

ADVICE RECORD

Date: _____   Hostess: _____

Guest

Advice

_____

_____

_____

_____

_____

_____

_____

_____

_____

_____

_____

_____

_____

ADVICE RECORD

Date: _____   **Hostess:** _____

Guest   **Advice**

_____   _____

                                    _____

_____   _____

                                    _____

_____   _____

                                    _____

_____   _____

                                    _____

_____   _____

ADVICE RECORD

Date: _____   Hostess: _____

Guest

Advice

_____

_____

_____

_____

_____

ADVICE RECORD

Date: _____   Hostess: _____

<table>
<tr><td align="center">**Guest**</td><td align="center">**Advice**</td></tr>
</table>

_____   _____

                                   _____

_____   _____

                                   _____

_____   _____

                                   _____

_____   _____

                                   _____

_____   _____

ADVICE RECORD

Date: _____   Hostess: _____

Guest   **Advice**

_____

_____   _____

_____

_____   _____

_____

_____   _____

_____

_____   _____

_____

ADVICE RECORD

Date: _____   Hostess: _____

Guest	Advice

ADVICE RECORD

Date: _____   Hostess: _____

Guest

Advice

_____

_____

_____

_____

_____

ADVICE RECORD

Date: _____   **Hostess:** _____

Guest	Advice

ADVICE RECORD

Date: _____   Hostess: _____

Guest   **Advice**

_____   _____

                                      _____

_____   _____

                                      _____

_____   _____

                                      _____

_____   _____

                                      _____

_____   _____

                                      _____

⁀Anniversaries

The bride can use this list of anniversary gift categories in the years to come.

1   *paper*

2   *cotton*

3   *leather*

4   *books, fruit, or flowers*

5   *wood or clocks*

6   *iron or candy*

7   *copper, bronze, brass, or wool*

8   *electrical appliances*

9   *pottery or willow*

10 *tin or aluminum*

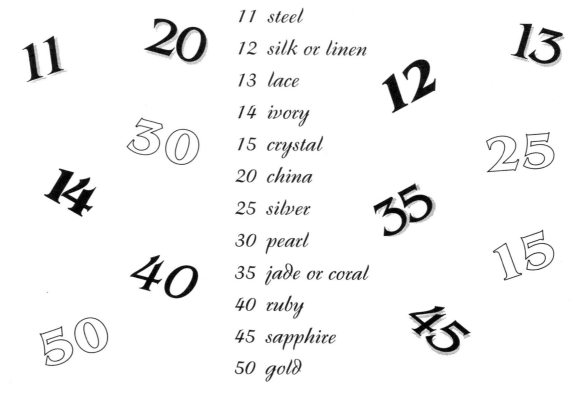

11 steel
12 silk or linen
13 lace
14 ivory
15 crystal
20 china
25 silver
30 pearl
35 jade or coral
40 ruby
45 sapphire
50 gold

ᵉIndex